FOR ENTREPRENEURS ONLY

A MENTOR'S GUIDEBOOK

FOR BUDDING ENTREPRENEURS

Vern Walden

Copyright © 2021 VERN WALDEN

All rights reserved.

ISBN9798532853256

FORWARD

Experience is the bridge between knowledge and wisdom. I am writing this guide out of my love for business, bridging knowledge and wisdom with my many business experiences. For all entrepreneurs, I wish you success and hope this guide is the grease that gets you there.

Vern Walden

Table of Contents

New product/service guidelines	I
Pricing your products	II
Product development	III
Rules for building a business	IV
Words of wisdom	V
About the author	VI

NEW PRODUCT (or service) GUIDELINES

1) Low start-up cost to bring to market or licensed

2) Disposable (requires repurchase)

3) Unique and/or better

4) Good margins/profit

5) Long product life with commodity potential.

6) Unexploited or under-exploited niche.

7) Potential for crossover into additional markets such as promotional or industrial/commercial.

8) Low product (or service) liability

9) Indefinite shelf life

10) Multiple product (or service) uses/customer niches

PRODUCTS/SERVICES SHOULD MEET AT LEAST 1-8 OF THE GUIDELINES FOR CONSIDERATION IN MOST NICHES.

I

PRICING YOUR PRODUCTS

Always price products to make a good living...not a killing.

Henry Ford strove to price his cars so the average person could afford one and, by 1929, 50% of all U.S. families had one!

General Pricing Formula: Wholesale or Retail

Asking price to customer minus your cost divided by asking price to customer = profit margin%.

Ex: Asking price $2, minus $1 your cost, divided by $2 asking price = 50% margin   A higher margin means more profit/less work.

Multiplying 2 times your cost as an asking price to customer = 50% profit margin, 3 times = 66% profit margin, 4 times = 75% profit margin.

PRODUCT DEVELOPMENT

Product development and licensing can be a very viable and lucrative endeavor. In many cases, it may make more sense and mean less risk to license your product to another company rather than produce and market it yourself.

I don't recommend using 'product development companies' for prototypes, patents or promises of licensing deals. These are things you can do for a fraction of the cost of a 'product development company' with better results.

Protecting your idea: Product development and licensing is high risk but is also high reward. The key to reducing risk (money & time) is to file a PPA (provisional patent). This will give you one year from the filing date to license your product. The filing fee is under $100 (at time of this writing) for a micro-entity. Trademarks and copyrights can also be very valuable.

Go to the uspto.gov website for more information, forms and guidelines.

It is important to use a nondisclosure agreement (NDA) when disclosing an idea to others. If you don't have a well-written NDA signed before disclosing an idea, you will be putting your intellectual property into the public domain.

Low risk/start-up cost is the path to any business or product development success. I believe in using contract manufacturers/subcontractors for everything you can't do yourself. This method will reduce your risk (money & time). You will discover with many unproven ideas, they will fail. Therefore, use your resources wisely (treasure, time, talent).

VERN'S 20 RULES FOR BUILDING A BUSINESS

1. Cash flow is everything.

2. Keep inventory to a minimum...don't buy inventory on spec. Buy inventory as needed/or JIT (just in time). Things are cheaper in quantity but it's not cheap when you can't sell it/move it and have to warehouse it. Don't have $$ sitting in inventory.

3. Look at debt as toxic/poison to your business. The healthiest businesses are the ones out of debt.

4. Finance your growth by using your vendors' net (30-60) payment and customers with cash/upfront payment. Do not offer credit, if possible.

5. With cash on hand you can take advantage of good

deals (computers/equipment) and, even at times, inventory. Cash is always king.

6. Run your business out of your home, if possible. (see #14) If you have a dedicated space for business-use-only in your home, you may be able to use it as a tax deduction; check with an accountant or IRS for rules.

7. Using consulting services to speed progress is expensive and they mostly provide 'conventional wisdom' and gimmicks that, in time, generally do not work to accelerate your progress.

8. Always negotiate prices of goods and services when possible. Dollars saved go on the bottom line as profit. Ex: Advertising is experimental and costly. Use as many free methods (website, video channels, word-of-mouth, press releases, etc.) as you can.

9. Leases can be dangerous. Important! If you must

have an outside space, take on a short-term lease for an unproven business model. If the business fails and you break the lease, you will be on the hook for the payment until the space is leased to someone else (and/or whatever is in the terms of your lease re: penalties, etc.).

10. Shipping charges can reduce your margins as much as 10% or more if you are paying for shipping. I always try to use local/nearby vendors and subcontractors to reduce this cost.

11. The three resources needed in most business are land, labor and capital. I always eliminated land and labor by subcontracting our business needs, thus reducing risk. Your part of the business is creator, investor and micro-manager.

12. Most franchises are high-risk businesses that require large start-up capital. You will also be on the hook for a royalty fee on sales and lease payments (for

bricks & mortar retail).

13. Partners and investors can reduce your financial risk up front. But, you are giving up control. Control/independence is the main reason for self-employment. Therefore, if you take on partners/investors, never give up more than 49% ownership in the business. If you have a minority ownership (less than 50%) you could be paying to have a job...not to mention the emotional stress.

14. Great--Subcontractors! I love subcontractors because of fixed costs for producing a product or service you need. Using subcontractors will eliminate land and labor, reserving capital. I shipped products to international chains like Wal-Mart and others from an in-home office using subcontractors for everything from manufacturing, to warehousing, packaging and shipping.

There are special needs jobbers for packaging and shipping (like Goodwill) and you will be employing people who need jobs and do excellent work!

15. I do not recommend taking on investors to build your business. You will be taking on partners and will lose some or most control. Even worse, with family members as investors, if the business fails and you aren't able to repay their investment (if that is part and parcel of your agreement) it will cause a multitude of relationship problems. I have heard 'family investor horror stories'.

16. Always give the customer more than they expect; for example, samples of something else in your line or, in the case of food items, recipes to use.

17. It's good to know a little about income tax. Every year, I purchase an inexpensive tax software program and, with my gross sales number, I run a model with my expenses on Schedule C to see if I could increase my expenses or not, if need be.

18. I have no experience in buying an existing business; therefore, I will only say – use caution -- go over the records with a fine-toothed comb. As well, if possible, seek information from someone in business who has purchased a business(es) for guidance.

19. Business is mostly about risk/reward. Every idea/business takes time, up to a decade or even longer, to develop to its' fullest. So, be careful what you run with.

20. Don't use all your resources at the beginning. Set aside resources for a backup plan aka 'Plan B' if circumstances require one…and always have an exit strategy.

*   *   *   *   *

I hope you have gained information in this booklet that will help you get started in marketing your product/service/ideas.

Much of what you do will still be 'trial and error'. However, if you use the information in this booklet, you should save time and money and avoid disastrous mistakes.

All the best as you embark on a tremendous, frustrating, exciting, fun, exhausting, exhilarating journey!

Vern

WORDS OF WISDOM

An entrepreneur is:

A generator of jobs

A creator of wealth

A contributor to society

It's easy to create something complicated. It's hard to create something simple.

On partnerships: Put one person in charge and progress continues. Put two people in charge and progress stops.

Money is much easier to spend than it is to make.

Learn from others, but experience is still the best teacher.

Big dreams make for big battles.

Live to give. (treasure, time, talent)

Will the juice be worth the squeeze? (reward vs. risk)

Learn to be a problem solver.

Learn to be a producer – not a consumer.

Learn to be a giver – not a taker.

Change is painful but, without it, there is no gain.

Use adversity as an opportunity to find creative solutions to problems.

Be best, not cheapest.

Do what you do best and delegate the rest.

ABOUT THE AUTHOR

A) Past co-owner of a real estate brokerage in Southern California. Owned rental properties and flipped investment property.

B) Had a wholesale clip-strip business with customers including Wal-Mart, K-Mart, Meijer and a number of other chains and distributors.

C) Did all R&D for retail start-up. Owner of local retail business (bricks and mortar) for many years.

D) Developed and licensed an invention to the beverage industry (commercial equipment).

E) Have run an online business for years selling a food product.

F) Author of a previous business start-up guide/booklet and have helped others start successful businesses.

www.ingramcontent.com/pod-product-compliance
Lightning Source LLC
Chambersburg PA
CBHW070916220526
45466CB00005B/2240